BIG YIELDS, LITTLE POTS

BIG YIELDS, LITTLE POTS

*Container Gardening
for the Creative Gardener*

The Hungry Garden series #1

Rosefiend Cordell

Rosefiend Publishing.

Ordering information: For details, contact the publisher at hello@melindacordell.com
Cover design by Melinda R. Cordell
Book formatting by Melinda R. Cordell

ISBN: 978-1-953196-29-3

First Edition: July 2020

10 9 8 7 6 5 4 3 2 1 blast off!

For more information (and books!), visit my website at
https://melindacordell.com/

The Hungry Garden Series

Just to say 'Thank You' for purchasing this book, I want to give you a gift.

Perennial Classics: Planting & Growing Great Perennial Gardens from my Easy-Growing Gardening series.
<u>Click here to access your free gift!</u>
https://melindacordell.com/subscribe/

Do you have a gardening story you'd like to share? Tell me your experience with container gardening (or any other gardening stories) at <u>hello@melindacordell.com</u>! If it fits the topic, I might use it (with your permission and correct attribution, of course) in one of my future books.

Table of Contents

INTRODUCTION

Container Gardening for the Rest of Us

THIS BOOK IS ABOUT GROWING vegetables, berries, herbs, and edible flowers in a variety of containers, and will cover all the details you need to know to succeed in this endeavor. Now, I have to tell you that container gardening is not going to support a whole family (unless you really, really, *really* go to town with these pots) but container garden can supplement your diet in all the best ways.

If you have come to this book looking for pretty design ideas, I'm afraid you're going to be disappointed. My landscaping style, if you're generous, could be considered shabby chic – but to this country girl, it's probably a lot closer to redneck lite, which means it's a little rough around the edges but perfectly serviceable. (If my landscaping style were full-on redneck, then there'd be an old car parked in the middle of my garden.)

However! If your main objective in picking up this book is to grow a truckload of vegetables in a bunch of pots, then you're in the right place.

I've worked in horticulture for half of my life – longer if you count when I was young. I started learning how to identify wildflowers when I was in fifth grade. When I was a freshman in high school, I'd sit in the library reading Steyermark's *Flora of Missouri*, not for any class assignments, but for FUN. When I was a high school senior in 1989, I got my first plant-related job at a small-town garden center. (I also worked as a newspaper carrier and church pianist.)

Since then, I've worked in retail and commercial greenhouses, as a landscape laborer and designer, as a perennials manager, and as a municipal horticulturist and public rose garden potentate. When I was city horticulturist, I took care of 36 gardens and a bunch of trees, shrubs, roses, over I don't know how many square miles of city. I had a schedule that I really had to try and stick to, because if I didn't, I ended up with a train wreck of unfinished chores and as a result, all the gardens suffered.

These days, I work as a gardening author – which is much easier on the back and joints. After all these years of working in 95-degree summer heat, I really, really, *really* love air conditioning.

My books are written out of three decades' experience with the plant world. I write out of a deep understanding of plants and how to grow them, and I do my best to keep updating my knowledge, so I can pass on the best information I can, while making it fun.

Me in my horticulturing days, lying in front of the fan and trying to cool off after a 95-degree day (Marcus is the awesome little dog there)

A Rule of Thumb (green or otherwise)

Here's a little thing to remember: Keeping plants contented and blossoming and fruiting takes a certain skillset – and this skillset *can* be learned.

I've heard a lot of people say, self-deprecatingly, "Oh, I have a brown thumb." I don't think that's true at all. Gardening is simply as a series of learning experiences, just as any new discipline is. If you hang out in the kitchen and cook things, eventually you learn how to cook good food. If you sit at the piano every day and practice, eventually you learn to play piano. You're not going to play like Rachmaninoff (that's a whole 'nother level of work), but if you enjoy it, that's all right.

The same rules apply to gardening. If something doesn't work this year, well, just try something different next year. Patience, observation, and a willingness to learn new things are among the best tools you can have in your gardening toolbox (and these tools serve you well in many other areas in life).

In short, a green thumb isn't something you're born with: It's something you learn. If it's any consolation, I've had many plants croak on me through the years, and I'll have more keel over on me in the future. But I keep learning better ways to grow plants, and even now, I'm learning new things. If I can do it, so can you.

I've loaded this book with all the information you'll need to plant a container garden. You'll learn about the types of containers you can use (and their pros and cons) and I've included a primer about soilless potting mix and how to start seeds. The bulk of these chapters will be about the different food crops you can grow in pots – the best varieties of each vegetable for containers, and how to successfully grow them all. I hope you enjoy.

When you get done reading, please leave an honest review for this book on Amazon, BookBub, or Goodreads.

Reviews are so helpful to authors and to the readers who are looking for good books.

PART I

GET STARTED WITH CONTAINER GARDENING

The Whys and Wherefores

SO, WHY PLANT YOUR VEGETABLES in containers?

Maybe you don't have yard space, or even a yard, to plant in.

Perhaps you have hardpan soil, or soil that's high in lead, or what I call "subdivision soil," that gummy subsoil churned up from construction.

Perhaps your husband is a lawn fiend who cannot imagine his kingdom of grass having one plant out of place in it, bless his heart. Or maybe you're planting food for only one.

Maybe you want to plant something tasty within reach of your back door. Or you want to keep your food up on the deck, the only place where the chipmunks won't dig up all your vegetables, the little nitwits.

Or maybe you have limited mobility, or can't grip gardening implements, or you might be experiencing those myriad difficulties that slow us down.

There are a ton of reasons why growing your vegetables in containers will work for you. Containers can be raised and lowered to be within reach, and can be kept where they're easily accessible so you can avoid pain or exhaustion while you work.

Whatever your reasons, this is the book for you.

Container gardening can have its challenges. Sometimes pots get knocked over. Sometimes you leave home for a week, and return to find that a full-scale drought and extreme heat have shriveled up your plants. It happens.

Protip: Don't shoot for perfection when it comes to gardening. Perfection = frustration.

The nice thing about container gardening is how versatile it is. If you don't like how one of your plants look, you can move it elsewhere; if a plant isn't getting enough sun, you can scoot it into a sunnier patch; if the arrangement of your containers doesn't please you, you can rearrange them to your heart's content. You might have to water daily when it gets hot and dry outside, but if you're able to set up a drip watering system, you can circumvent that. Weeds are much, much, *much* easier to handle with container gardening, as are insects. If one of your plants looks mopey, you can move it out of sight to your plant hospital to recuperate while you put a cheery-looking plant in its place.

And here's something to remember in gardening, or just in life in general:

IT'S PERFECTLY OKAY TO BREAK THE RULES.

Your garden is not going to be perfect. Oftentimes it doesn't even have to be right. If you have some extra plants, crowd them into a pot somewhere. If you can't follow the fertilizing directions exactly, do your best. If you don't have money to get fancy pots, get some five-gallon buckets or make do with something cheap. Don't spend a lot of money trying to make your containers look like garden porn out of a magazine.

Seriously, if *Better Homes and Gardens* showed up to photograph my backyard, I'd have to chase them off with a broom. (After all these years of horticulturing, I have grown to absolutely despise weeding with the heat of ten thousand suns.) Now, see? You're already way ahead of me.

Just plant things. Enjoy the work. That's going to be the takeaway in this book.

Go Organic

You're likely going to have a number of crops in pots ripening at different times through the growing season. That means you'll need pollinators to visit your plants for most of the summer (because as you know, Bob, this whole growing operation works best with cooperation from pollinators). Using organic pest control on your plants will be the best way to grow healthy produce while keeping your pollinators safe.

If you must spray, do it in the late afternoon or evening, after pollinators go home for the night. And use several means of control along with spraying. Often people will spray and consider the work done, only to be discouraged by seeing that the infestation hasn't gone away. Some insects will survive being sprayed, but almost none of them will survive being squished.

I once had a mealybug problem on a potted plant in the greenhouse. Mealybugs are tough to eradicate. These are tiny white insects with a water-resistant (and pesticide-resistant) waxy coat. They will congregate on stems, underneath leaves, and have a penchant for packing themselves into the spaces where the leaf meets the stem, where it's hard to squish and spray them, where they can sip plant juices undisturbed. The females lay egg masses covered with a water (and pesticide) resistant cottony coat, and they excrete sticky honeydew everywhere.

Mealybugs – courtesy of Q. Holdman, ARS-USDA

I put a systemic pesticide in the soil so the plant would absorb the poison into its juices, trying to kill the mealybugs that way. They just drank up the poisonous plant juice. I sprayed the mealybugs repeatedly with pyrethrum, but they just put up little umbrellas and kept multiplying.

So I started squishing them. I looked for them in every hiding place on the plant. I squished their tiny nymphs and the egg masses and any bugs I could find, and I did this daily. I even found a few under the soil near the surface, on the plant roots. I also kept spraying pyrethrum to pick off the insects I missed. Finally the mealybug numbers dwindled until they were all gone, and the plant unfurled new leaves and started growing again.

For best results, fight the war on several fronts.

ALL ABOUT CONTAINERS

The Good, the Bad, the Ugly

A SOLID AND HANDSOME CONTAINER can make container gardening and enjoyable enterprise, while a bad container can be a headache. If the pot's too small, you get a rootbound plant. When the pot's too big, you use a lot of potting soil only to have a dinky plant sitting in the middle, looking lonely. Here's a list of considerations to guide you through the container-choosing process.

You'll want a container to be tough and durable because you don't want to bump against a pot and have it fall apart. Accidents do happen.

Always have drainage holes in your containers. I've found that pots will drain best if your holes are wider than a pencil. If the drainage hole is not allowing water to drain out, get your widest drill bit and widen the hole as much as possible.

You don't want to leave water sitting in the bottom of the pot, giving your plant waterlogged roots. If you let a pot without a drainage hole fill up with water, you'll regret it. When you tip the pot over and let the putrid water run out, the stink will make your eyes water!

Large containers do best with several drainage holes. If the drainage hole is super-huge, you can cover it with a coffee filter, plastic screening, a piece of landscape fabric, shards from a broken flowerpot, or large rocks to keep the potting soil from running out with the water. Also, raise the pot off the ground for best drainage, using pot feet, a pot cart, or a couple of bricks.

A container should be moveable, if possible. I used to have large pots of hibiscus trees in my greenhouse, and they were a pain to move. Then somebody made a back-saving suggestion: Put Styrofoam packing peanuts at the bottom of the pot. They would help with drainage and they'd keep the pot light. I did as they suggested, and it was so much easier to move the pots around after that.

(Be sure you don't use biodegradable packing peanuts in your pots. These will slowly melt away as you keep watering the plant – and you probably don't want to see your tomato plant slowly sinking into the pot as they do.)

You can also use crushed aluminum cans or plastic milk jugs to lighten a heavy pot. Put your layer of lightweight materials into the bottom of the pot, lay a strip of landscape fabric over the top of them, then pour the potting soil on top. This saves money, because filling a pot completely with potting soil can end up being pricey. Modify this if you are growing a small tree, which might be top-heavy in a lightweight pot.

Choosing the Right Pot

One important aspect of gardening is knowing how big your plants are going to get so you can fit them into the right-sized spot.

Small lettuces can be planted in a row in a long, narrow container, while a dwarf apple tree will need a large container that will contain its roots while not overcrowding them. When growing tomatoes in containers, it's better to choose a determinate tomato plant, which stays small. An indeterminate tomato, on the other hand, will take over your deck like Godzilla, if Godzilla happened to bear tasty red fruits.

If you're not sure how big your container should be for your plant, you should be all right getting one that is two or three inches larger in diameter than the original pot it came in. That will give your plant room enough to stretch out its roots. (Of course, if you buy a plant in one of those little two-inch pots, do get a pot that's larger than four inches.) A mature rootball on a plant can be surprisingly large, so choose your pots accordingly.

If you have carrots, use a deep pot with light, fluffy soil.

Upright, bushy plants such as tomatoes, peppers, and eggplants like a four to five-gallon container.

A pot that's eight inches deep is good for root vegetables and climbing vegetables. Window boxes are good for salad greens.

If you're trying to choose between two pots, one larger than the other, always go with the larger pot if you can. You generally need more pot than you think. (And if your plant does end up being too small, you can tuck some other plants around her to fill in some space.)

PROTIP:
IT'S PERFECTLY OKAY TO BREAK THE RULES.

And this applies to the eternal conundrum of "How many plants should I put into one pot?"

Go out into any forest, or grassy field, or any wild area, and just spend some time looking at the plants.

What rules are these wildflowers and grasses following? Are they social distancing at all? How close are the trees in the forest? Do they space themselves out at all?

The gardening space guidelines that I'm giving are only there to help you give each plant the space they need to prosper in the garden. But a plant might grow one way in certain conditions and then grow another way in a different location. Plants are living things, and like most living things can be contrary.

Space guidelines are to give you guidance so you don't plant your trees too close to the house, or plant your

13

rosebushes so close that you can't get through them. But guidelines aren't hard and fast rules.

If you have limited garden space and you want to cram a few extra plants into a container, do it. Create a big, glorious mess. If things go haywire, pull up some extra plants to open up some space. Be sure to mix different species together for the best results in chumminess – and if some plants are bad neighbors, make a note of it and don't mix them together next year.

I'll give size recommendations for pots and numbers of plants, but remember that you can still throw stuff together in pots any old which way. To paraphrase Martin Luther, "Sin bravely, and see how much of God's grace you can get!"

(Nothing egregious, mind you. I suppose this means that I sin timidly.)

For those of you who prefer to play by the rules, here are some ballpark numbers for pot sizes.

24-inch pot:
A big pepper plant

Summer squash

Pumpkin

Indeterminate tomato (with a cage that fits in the pot)

(Protip: These four plants above will appreciate a pot that's wide AND deep.)

Cucumber

Artichoke

A mix of small veggies and herbs can be planted around the edges to fill in.

18-inch pot
Broccoli

Cauliflower
Large cabbage
Small eggplant
A crapload of greens
Small pepper plant
Determinate tomato (with little cage)

14-inch pot
Herbs!
A not-so-large cabbage
Collards
Three or four spinach
Three or four non-heading lettuce
Three arugula (Arugulas? Arugulae?)

10-inch pot
Single herb plant
A strawberry plant
A few lettuce plants

Lettuce and other shallow-rooted plants prefer wider containers over taller ones.

Picture (and balcony garden!) by Ico Ahyicodae

A Primer of Container Materials

So which containers are great for container gardening? Which ones aren't worth a plugged nickel? Here's a quick rundown.

DIY Containers

In container gardening, the old mainstay is the five-gallon bucket, which is cheap or even free, and it has its own useful handle. Or you can create unusual containers from items that are sitting around your house, and you're limited only by your ingenuity. You can make containers for your plants out of old sinks, bathtubs, used tires, straw bales, boots, wash tubs, and kiddie swimming pools. I believe this is called "upcycling." If you do this with a designer's eye, then you can be trendy and call it "shabby chic." If you're not interested in being trendy you can call it your redneck garden. Whatever you call it, your containers are limited only by your

16

imagination – and, for you unlucky souls, the rules of your homeowner's association.

Wooden

Speaking of shabby chic, rustic wooden containers look nice and are sturdy. Half-whisky barrels have long been a popular choice for being functional and enduring. Wooden containers are semi-porous, so they allow some air into the soil (this is a good thing). Wood eventually deteriorates over time, so line it with plastic to slow the process. (Make sure there's a hole in the plastic for drainage.)

Be sure the wood has not been treated with preservatives, which can get into the soil and your plants, and be sure that it has not been treated with creosote, which can get all over you if you're within a two-mile radius of it.

Terracotta

The orange terracotta pots are the quintessential flowerpot. These are popular, tidy, cheap, are available in all sizes, and the orange color contrasts nicely with the green leaves.

Drawbacks: Terracotta can crack or break, and you can't leave these pots outside over winter because the freeze/thaw cycle will crack them. The large terracotta pots can be heavy and hard to move. Because the clay is porous, it allows air to reach the soil, but it also allows water to wick out, so the plants in these pots will need to be watered more often.

Ceramic and Pottery

These are available in an incredible array of colors, shapes, and sizes. Naturally, these will cost more, but you can find some stunning pieces that add delicious colors and forms to your surroundings. It's amazing what beauty these potters can create from clay, slip, glaze, and fire.

Like terracotta, pottery is also porous and can dry out quickly, so plants in pottery and ceramic pieces will likely need to be watered more often. Also like terracotta, these pots should be brought in for the winter so they are not cracked by sudden freezes. However, there are frost-resistant ceramics available that look great and can be left out through the winter.

Plastic and Fiberglass

These are also available in an array of styles and sizes. Plastic pots are non-porous, so they won't need to be watered as often. Do be sure (as with any pot) that these have drainage holes so your plants don't end up swimming in the soil. Plastic containers are cheaper, lightweight, hard to break, and easier to move.

Storage Containers

If you are more interested in crop production than aesthetics, then plastic storage containers make great places to grow vegetables.

Here's how to repurpose them. Drill several drainage holes into the bottoms of the storage containers. Fill the bottom of the container with pumice or Styrofoam peanuts to make the container lightweight (and so you don't use so much potting soil). Then plant. Put the lid underneath the container to catch water, and raise the container slightly off the lid with a few thin pieces of wood or stone – this allows the water to drain out.

Algae will grow inside clear plastic containers where the sun hits them, so if you don't like the resulting flush of green, engineer some way to keep them in the shade.

Stone

Stone containers are super-beautiful! And they're super-heavy! Stone has similar pros and cons to ceramics, as far as beauty and frost breakability. Stone heats up quickly in the sun – a great thing in cool climates, but a problem in desert climates.

Wood Pulp and Coco Coir

Wood pulp pots look like they're made lumpy cardboard. We used to get our one-gallon perennials in these kinds of pots, which were earth-friendly, because you could compost those things after you got your plants in the ground. (You can plant the smaller pulp pots directly into the ground if you first cut them up so the roots can get out.) Wood pulp pots aren't good long-term containers, since they will break down readily.

Wood pulp and coconut coir are often used as liners for hanging baskets. Hanging baskets made of coir look nice, but water will drain straight through them, and they dry out in about five seconds. When I was city horticulturist, a local association had hanging baskets installed all through downtown. This was fine, except they insisted on using coir baskets in summer, and those things dried out fast. I was out there three times a week watering those things, and it still wasn't enough to keep the plants hydrated.

Finally I put a bunch of moisture-retaining crystals in the soil of each basket so I could spend more time on all my other gardens and the millions of chores that needed to be done around the city. These crystals, which are mixed into the soil, are made of polymers that absorb water and swell into something that resembles a tiny block of gelatin. Plants will send their roots straight to these tiny water reservoirs. These moisture-retaining crystals are good for only one season, but they helped keep the Wave petunias alive. Thus I was able to stay within the good graces of the Downtown Association, mostly.

Hanging Baskets

The ultimate space-saving option, just as long as you can hang them in a spot where you don't bang your head on them 14 times a day. Hanging baskets are good for trailing plants like cherry tomatoes, herbs, and strawberries. Since they're suspended in the air, they will of course dry out faster and will need to be watered daily or every other day. Naturally, I recommend plastic pots, mainly because I was scarred for life by the Sisyphean task of endlessly watering coir baskets all over downtown St. Joseph.

PART II
CONTAINER GROWING BASICS

All the Useful Info You Need

As you know, there's more to gardening than just plunking a plant in a pot and saying "Okay, bub, now start growing." Which the plant will do anyway, whether you tell it to or not.

So what's the best gardening soil for containers? How do you start seeds? How much should we water? How can we keep these plants contented and growing?

Well, dive in and we'll get started.

STARTING SEEDS IN CONTAINERS

*Swiped and amended from **If You're a Tomato I'll Ketchup With You** .*

Starting plants from seed has always been a fun activity. From browsing the colorful seed catalogs, to seeing the new shoots breaking the soil, to enjoying the harvest of these once tiny plants – it's amazing how you can get five hundred pounds of zucchini from a tiny seed.

If you start your plants from seed, it's best to start them inside in late winter, whether on a windowsill or in a cold frame. At any rate, many seeds need a soil temperature of at least 60 degrees to germinate, though some prefer warmer temperatures, up to 80 degrees.

You can start some of your seeds under lights as early as February. Then, when the weather is mild enough, transplant the young plants to their designated container outside, using sheets or mulch protect the plants against surprise frosts and freezes.

So get out your calendar, count back six or eight weeks from your frost date, and that's the date you sow your seeds. (Protip: Keep a gardening calendar and notebook where you write down things like sowing dates, the dates you see frost, etc. Then you can use this information next winter when you're planning for the upcoming planting year.)

Next, line up your planting containers. Seedling containers can be made with all kinds of found containers. Used food containers work well, as well as yogurt containers and toilet paper tubes with the bottom folded up.

Milk jugs cut in half make great seedling containers. Cut off the bottom of the milk jug, punch drainage holes in it, put in the potting soil, then add in the seeds and cover with soil. Put the top of the milk jug back to hold the moisture in as the seedlings germinate. Rotisserie chicken containers and clear salad containers also are great for starting seedlings.

Whether you use old egg cartons, Solo cups, or flowerpots, wash them with hot water, soap, and a dash of bleach. Cleaning up the trays/flowerpots will clean up any diseases that might be harbored there – diseases that could affect young seedlings.

Be sure that, whatever you use, your planter has plenty of drainage holes! This is not negotiable!

How to Plant Seeds

When sowing seeds, it's best to use a light seeding mix that is high in vermiculite. This kind of seeding mix is lighter and easier for newly-germinated seedlings to poke their little green heads through. However, a regular "soilless" potting mix works fine in a pinch.

When I ran the city greenhouse, I always started my seedlings in trays. I'd pour a scoop or so of moistened seeding mix into the tray and tamp it down – the guys at work made a really nice tamp for me out of a piece of wood that fit the length of the tray with a handle on it, so I'd spread out the soil, flatten it, and sprinkle in the seeds.

The late George Ferbert, who owned greenhouses in St. Joseph, Missouri, for years and years, showed me a little trick when seeding flats: He'd add a little bit of sugar to the seeds before he sowed them. The sugar shows up against the black dirt so you can see where the seeds land, so you can broadcast them more evenly around the surface of the soil. Lobelia seeds are tinier than even the sugar crystals. When I added a little sugar to the cup of seeds to "see where they hit," the sugar crystals stick out of the Lobelia seeds like boulders in sand.

At any rate, when you mix the tiny seeds with a half-teaspoon of sugar, that helps the seeds scatter out, keeps them from clumping, and you can see where the seeds and sugar fall into the soil. You will have to keep mixing the sugar and seeds as you sow, because the two substances will not stay evenly mixed. Fine sand also works with tiny seeds. You can use this method whether you're sowing the seeds scattershot or in neat rows.

If you prefer to plant seeds in rows, take a #2 pencil, dab the point lightly into water and wipe it off, then touch the pencil to the seed to pick it up. Then you can use the pencil as your dibble – that is, use the pencil to make the hole and plant the seeds.

Once the seeds are sown, shake ¼ or ½ of soil over the top of the seeds, depending on the depth the seed packet recommends, gently tamp the soil down, and water. I used a super-fine spray head on my watering wand, taking care not to let the water puddle in the tray. If you can find a watering can with a super-fine spray head on it, you're set.

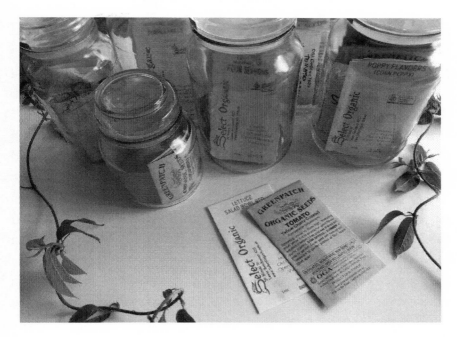

For those of you with a small-scale operation, seeding is a little less involved. Fill your pots, cups, etc. with potting mix, leaving about a half-inch to an inch at the top. Poke two or three seeds into the middle, about a quarter-inch deep, and cover them. (You're planting two seeds just in case one doesn't sprout.) When they get bigger, pinch out the wimpier seedling and let the larger one grow.

Gently pack the soil in around the seeds, because seed-to-soil contact is important for good germination rates.

Sprinkle water on the soil, and keep the soil moist. Dry soil will kill the seedlings, and constantly wet soil will rot them.

One way to keep the soil from drying out is to cover the trays or pots with plastic wrap. If you use plastic wrap, don't leave the trays in direct sunlight. One time I had the soil covered this way on one of my flats. I came in from one of my jobs and realized that it had been sitting in the sun all afternoon. I ran over and lifted up the plastic wrap – and steam puffed out. Those seeds were roasted!

Seeds will germinate more effectively if you have a heat mat under the cups or trays. This will warm the soil with dependable heat, allowing the seedlings to germinate and grow out more quickly. Just be sure to get a thermostat with the mats so you can adjust the temperature so you don't end up cooking your seeds.

Once the seeds germinate, be sure to remove the plastic wrap, and have a small fan to keep the air circulating around them. Seedlings are susceptible to a disease called "damping off" which is encouraged by poor air circulation.

Damping-Off Disease

Back when I was a city horticulturist, I had a bout of damping-off disease in my greenhouse, and it was a mess. Damping-off is a fungal disease that causes newly-planted seedlings to keel over at soil level and melt away. It spreads out in a circle, as most funguses do (consider "fairy rings," which are circles of mushrooms on the forest floor), killing off seedlings as it spreads outward.

I hadn't experienced damping-off disease before, since I kept the soil on the dry side in the greenhouse, which the fungus didn't like.

That all changed after a whole week of cloudy, cold weather. My trays of seedlings, watered on a Sunday, would not dry out for the rest of the week. The sun refused to come out, and I couldn't turn on the fans to pull the air through for very long because it was too cold outside. Humidity was high. All the conditions were right for the fungus to strike.

Then the disease got into the snapdragons I'd just planted and started knocking them out everywhere. I got on the phone and called everyone I could think of for help. Then I took their advice, and it worked.

The best defense is a good offense. Keep a fan running at all times to keep the air circulating. You should feel the air moving through the whole room, but you don't have to turn it up so high that it blows the mice out from under the floor. Space the plants out to let air circulate between them. The fungus likes high humidity and temperatures about 70 degrees. The fan keeps the humidity and temperature lower.

This will break your heart, but get rid of everything that's been infected by the fungus. Dump out the soil and the plants with them, and take the waste outside so spores won't reinfect the plants. As soon as you see the seedlings keel over, and you know that it's not due to being underwatered, out they go.

If it's a really valuable tray of seedlings, you might dig out the infected plants, isolate the tray from all the other plants, turn a fan on them, try a soil drench of Captan fungicide (follow label directions), and keep your fingers crossed.

Once the seedlings are big enough to handle, you can transplant them into pots or four-packs. If you have a small windowsill operation, this won't be necessary. You can put some soil in a small Solo cup (with drainage holes poked into the bottom), stick two or three seeds in there, and let 'em grow until they're big enough to transplant directly into the garden.

Photo by Zoe Schaeffer. They are using a knife as a dibble to transplant seedlings – I always used an old pencil, as it was more comfortable in my hand. Use what suits you best.

Hardening Off Seedlings

Once the seedlings get big and husky, and once the weather warms up outside, it's time to harden off the seedlings so they can get acclimated to the weather. Plants do better if they have a little time to adjust to the cold temperatures, and the sun, and the wind.

About a week or two before planting them, start moving them outside for a little while. On the first couple of days, set them outside in the shade in a protected, warm area for an hour or two, then bring them back inside. Then slowly increase exposure to the sun and wind, leaving them outside for three hours, or four. Then, when you are close to planting time, leave them outside overnight several times (but only if the temperature is supposed to stay over 50 degrees all night).

28

While you're hardening them off, keep an eye on the plants to make sure they're not wilting or drying out.

Once they're back inside, reduce the amount of water you give them, and don't fertilize them until you plant them in the garden.

Don't worry if you miss a day, and don't stress about "not doing it right." Plants are often tougher than we give them credit for, and often there's no real "right way" or "wrong way." Sometimes regular life gets in the way, so if you can't put your seedlings out daily, it's okay. They'll forgive you.

Soilless Mixes

I REMEMBER WHEN I WAS WORKING in a greenhouse and being completely boggled when I first heard the term "soilless mix."

"This isn't soil?" I thought. No, young Jedi, the stuff in your plant pots isn't actually soil at all.

Soilless mixes have been developed over decades to enhance drainage and aeration in pots. They often consist of a mix of vermiculite, peat, bark, ground coconut hulls (coir fiber), perlite, and other materials. This makes potting medium is lightweight and easy to handle. It's springy so it won't become compacted. It allows valuable oxygen to reach the roots without drying them out, and lets water drain easily away.

Different mixes and percentages of these soilless mixes have been created for different plants. Succulents prefer a medium that doesn't hold moisture and drains well, so a soilless mix for these might contain more bark, perlite, or sand. On the other hand, a fern would need a richer soil with more peat in it.

No matter how good the soil in your garden is, it won't work very well in a pot. The processes that keep garden soil light and friable – the earthworms aerating it, the organic material created by dead plants and animals, the small soil-dwelling insects and the microorganisms breaking the organic material down, and the fungi and bacteria helping the soil stick together in aggregates – all of these exist in garden soil (or should), but these wide-ranging processes that keep the soil healthy and full of nutrients can't be replicated in a pot. That's why garden soil used in a pot eventually becomes infertile and hard as a brick. This also goes for bagged topsoil, which is generally sedge peat. Soil straight out of the garden can contain weed seeds. This can be discouraging if you're using the soil to start seedlings.

Sometimes you bring in surprise guests with your garden soil. Pillbugs and other soil-dwelling critters are great in the garden. They're not so great when you bring your flowerpots into the house and the pillbugs come out to have a tiny pillbug party on the kitchen counter. I mean, they're cute, but still.

Pillbug party not actual size.

However, adding regular garden soil to your potting soil could increase its fertility and water retention – and, if your container garden is in a windy location, could make your pots heavy enough to not tip over. Mix about 25 percent garden soil into your soilless mix to stretch your potting soil and get more bang for your buck.

(Protip: If you own a greenhouse, then you already know to *never* use actual soil in your growing medium. Real soil contains diseases and fungus. Outdoors, in the garden, the soil ecosystem has checks and balances against these. But when these diseases get into your growing medium, they will run rampant in your potted plants. You can disinfect and disinfect, but once you get a disease in the greenhouse, you just about have to burn the whole place down in order to contain it.)

Elements of Potting Medium

So what commonly goes into soilless potting mix? Is a question that has always ... well, okay, it hasn't baffled mankind for ages, but this is useful information if you're mixing your own soil, or if you're endlessly curious about the world and simply like knowing things.

Sterilized Compost

Adding this to your soil is a good (and cheap) way to feed your plants. It increases the weight of your potting mix, so your potted carrots don't go whirling away every time a breeze puff across your deck. Figuring out the nutritional value of compost is a weary task, as every batch of compost is different. That's why I don't look at compost as a fertilizer that I can assign an N-P-K number to, but as a very fertile all-purpose soil amendment that's worth its weight in gold.

Vermiculite

This is created when mica, a common mineral, is superheated. Vermiculite retains water and nutrients for roots to absorb. It's often used in special potting mixes used for germinating seeds, in about a 30/70 mix of vermiculite and coir. Though light, vermiculite does not lighten or aerate the soil as well as perlite does. That's okay, because vermiculite has increased cation exchange – that is, it is able to capture and hold a lot of nutrients on its surfaces, and then release those nutrients to hungry plant roots. This magnetic ability also keeps nutrients from being leached away every time you water.

Peat Moss

Sphagnum peat moss, which is harvested from Canadian peat bogs, has been a mainstay of potting soils for ages, because of its amazing water-absorbing and soil-conditioning properties. Back in my early days I was always buying a small bale to dig it into my garden soil, but I always had to cut the bale open and let a water hose drip over it overnight to get it to absorb water so I wouldn't have a bunch of sneezy peat fibers flying around when I used it.

Lately, peat moss in potting soil has been replaced by coconut coir, which is a much more sustainable alternative with similar properties. Peat moss has been over-harvested from Scottish peat bogs for years, and though the Canadian sphagnum peat bogs are in better shape than their cousins across the ocean, harvesting the peat moss also releases a lot of carbon into the air. Coir is a better, more eco-friendly alternative.

Peat tends to dry out quickly, and once it's dry it floats around in the air. Back in 1996, on hot, windy days when I was potting plants at George Ferbert's greenhouse, George would have to come in with the sprayer hose and wet down the potting mix in the potting table. I'd blow my nose and get all these peat bits in my Kleenex. Apparently coir does not do this. A definite improvement.

Perlite

When you heat certain types of volcanic rock to about 1,800 degrees Fahrenheit, you get perlite, which is a light, white substance that looks like Styrofoam bits. It doesn't have any nutritional value to plants, but it lightens up the soil by adding much-needed aeration. It will float to the top of the soil when you water. Don't substitute Styrofoam for perlite, because perlite is eco-friendly but Styrofoam is … not.

Coconut Coir

Coir is an excellent, light soil conditioner that holds water like a sponge. It's a sustainable by-product of the coconut industry, made from the fibrous coconut husk. They used to throw the husk out until people realized how handy it actually was.

This stuff looks amazingly like garden soil, spongy and light. Coir doesn't make the mess that peat does. Unlike peat moss, which resists water as much as a seven-year-old boy at bathtime, coir is very absorbent, retaining up to ten times its weight in water. Coir doesn't contain nutrients (but neither does peat moss), so it will need to have slow-release fertilizers added to it when used as a potting medium.

Like peat moss, you can buy coir in bricks or bales that will need to be rehydrated before you can use them. Soak them in water, or let a water hose drip slowly over them overnight.

Sometimes off-brand coir can be salty, which is bad for plants, so it needs to be flushed with water. Use established suppliers to avoid this.

Bark

This is a specialty item for plants that require large air pockets in the soil, as some orchids do. You won't plant your vegetables in bark, though some potting mixes will include bits of bark to improve drainage and add air circulation in the soil. Bark will need to be watered more often, naturally, because of this.

Sand

Potting medium generally include the coarse, sharp, or builder sand. Sand makes the potting medium much heavier, filling up those air pockets. If you have a pot that falls over a lot, sand might be a good addition to your soil. Coarse sand improves drainage.

Side note: In potting mixes, sand helps with drainage, but when you add sand to clay garden soil, you get the opposite effect – it turns it into concrete!

Fertilizer

You should always add some kind of organic granular slow-release fertilizer to the potting mix to add fertility. The materials in soilless media are low in fertility, so it is imperative that you add your own. Osmocote is what I usually added to the soil I made in the greenhouse (we jokingly called it "birdseed"), though any slow-release complete fertilizer will work as well.

A number of good organic fertilizers make good additions to your potting soil. If you're planting tomatoes or peppers, add a cup of dolomitic limestone to your potting medium to add calcium.

Greensand is a good soil amendment that doesn't get a lot of press, but it should. It's made from undersea deposits made in the ocean a million years ago, and is high in potassium and contains of trace minerals. Bone meal contains calcium and phosphorus; blood meal contains nitrogen. Kelp meal is low in the N-P-K nutrients (nitrogen, phosphorus, and potassium) but it also includes micronutrients and growth hormones that plants love.

Making Your Own

If you're a real do-it-yourself gardener, or a greenhouse operator, it may be cheaper for you to buy all these ingredients separately, in bulk, and then mix them in your own preferred proportions.

Some smaller greenhouses mix large batches of soil in a concrete mixer. My city greenhouse was smaller, and I'd mix each batch of soil by a hand in a wheelbarrow. If you mix soil in bulk, here's a soil recipe from the University of Illinois Extension:

Shredded coconut coir (1 bushel)
Vermiculite (1 bushel)
Ground limestone (1¼ cups)
Phosphate fertilizer, either 0-20-0 (½ cup) or 0-45-0 (¼ cup)
Slow release granular fertilizer such as 5-10-5 (1 cup)

Sift the soilless mix through a screen of ½ inch hardware cloth to break up lumps. If you're using the soilless mix for seed germination, use a hardware cloth screen of ¼ inch for a finely-textured soil.

However you mix it, store the potting mix that you don't use in a watertight container, like a plastic trashcan with a lid.

Notes on Reusing Potting Soil

Can you reuse potting soil from year to year? In the home garden, if your plants have been relatively disease free, then yes – to a point. It's better for your plants if you add fresh potting soil to the pot so your plants can have fresh organic material. After a few years, the organic material in the soilless mix will break down, and you'll have to replace it. The potting soil also loses fertility over time, which is bad for your plants.

One final note: When you're potting up the plants in your containers or pots, leave an inch of space between the top of the soil and the top of the pot. This allows the water to collect in the pot while you're watering, instead of running right back out.

Fertilizer

As I noted earlier, the materials used in a soilless potting mix are low in fertility. And, unlike regular soil, the soil in your pot will not contain the myriad processes that create natural fertility in the soil – organic matter that dead materials add to the soil; the microorganisms that busily create food sources for each other and the plant roots, etc. Without these processes, all you have is just plain dirt in a pot with hungry roots!

Plant roots pick up many of the nutrients in your pot, but some nutrients leach out, i.e. are carried out of the soil by the waste water that ends up in the saucer. So, it's easy to exhaust the soil of nutrients.

Container plants benefit from a weekly fertilizing program that replenishes these nutrients. If you have perennial plants in containers, replace the top layer of soil with compost every year, or mix in some well-rotted manure or granular fertilizer. This allows nutrients to travel down to the plant roots with every watering.

Two weeks after you pot your plants, start watering your plants with liquid fertilizer such as fish emulsion, Miracle Gro, compost tea, or whichever fertilizer you prefer, at half strength every week.

Every 10 to 12 weeks, add another dose of slow-release granular fertilizer to your pots. Liquid fertilizers are taken up and quickly used by the plant, while the slow-release granular fertilizer will keep releasing nutrients. When using pelleted fertilizer, be sure to read and follow label directions. Too much fertilizer only wastes it, and too much of a good thing inevitably turns into a bad thing.

Fish emulsion is smelly but an excellent source of nitrogen and other nutrients. Compost tea contains a good mix of nutrients. Other organic liquid fertilizers include liquid seaweed or kelp (which have lots of micronutrients), humates, liquid earthworm castings, and manure tea.

Your Plant's Support System

Some of your container plants will need support: trellises, stakes, netting, twine, or cages. Tomatoes will need trellises and stakes; squashes can be grown up a trellis to save space. Put in the supports before you plant your crops to avoid damaging their roots. A teepee of bamboo stakes or long sticks will hold pole beans or peas. If you train your cucumbers up a nylon mesh net, their fruit will hang down and grow straight. Wooden and metal trellises look nice, while cattle paneling or hog wire is functional and very strong.

If you really want to save space, plant small crops, like root vegetables or leafy greens, around the base of your trellis plants. Another good match are quick-maturing vegetables, such as radishes, to fill in space around your large, slow-to-harvest plants. Radishes will be harvested by the time your squash plants start taking over their pot and balcony.

Climate Considerations

As you prepare to plant, find out how long your growing season is. If you live in the north, you'll have a shorter growing season than somebody who lives in the south, which means that you'll have to choose plants that have a shorter date to harvest. However, if you plant indoors and get your seedlings growing under lights before the frost date, then plant them out once the danger of frost has passed, you can extend your growing season.

Whether you live north, south, east, or west, check with your local University Extension to find out which planting times are best for your area, and when your frost dates are. They have all kinds of free pamphlets if you visit them in person, or you can find all kinds of valuable information on their website. Every state in the United States has a University Extension service, and most every county has an Extension agent. It's a valuable and very helpful resource for any gardener.

Temperature

Some plants stop producing vegetables when the weather gets super-hot. Tomatoes stop flowering when temperatures go over 90 degrees so this will affect yields. Conversely, once the first frost hits, your basil will turn black and croak unless you give it some protection against the cold. So keep those variables in mind.

If you're in a hot climate, your plants might need a little shade during the hottest parts of the afternoon, so place them accordingly. Also, in hot climates, it's best to avoid using metal or dark-colored containers that will collect the heat of the sun and bake the plant roots.

Protip: Double-pot your pots to keep them cooler when the heat is brutal. Slip a smaller pot into a larger one, then put wet sphagnum moss or newspaper between the pots. Every time you water your plants, water the filler as well. This will keep the inside pot cooler in the heat of the sun, and help keep the roots from cooking.

You cold-climate dwellers will have the opposite problem: trying to find a place to put the containers so sudden freezes won't kill your plants. Look for warm microclimates in your yard – say, against the south side of your house – to keep plants warm in spring or late fall, or have your blankets ready to throw over your containers when there's a frost warning.

Mulch is an effective insulator for both hot and cold climates. Add a layer of mulch to the pot to keep the moisture in, to keep roots cool in the summer sun, to keep roots protected in the event of frost, and to keep little weeds from popping up in the potting soil.

Sunlight

Also, consider the amount of sunlight your planting location gets. Most crop plants need at least six hours of full sun every day. The nice thing about containers is that you can move them to where the sunlight is. And if you notice one potted plant getting skinny and leggy as it tries to grow up to get more light, you can move it to a place where it can get that light.

We gardeners can sometimes overestimate how much light a garden spot gets. To get an idea of how much sun your garden area gets, step outside and photograph the sunlight on the ground every two or three hours through the day, especially if you have trees or buildings nearby. (Keep in mind, too, that this spot will see different amounts of sun through the year. In winter, the sun hangs low in the south as it passes through the sky; in summer, it stays higher in the sky.) Naturally, if you have an open field with no trees or buildings around, this won't be a concern.

Protip: To make the best of your locations, put your large plant pots on wheeled caddies so you can roll them from place to place.

Wind

If you get severe summer storms, or have winds that come sweeping down the plain, take this into consideration when you're choosing pots and plants. Use shorter pots that are not top-heavy. Secure your plants and trellises to a railing or a wall, so you won't go outside some morning and find all your pots have toppled like dominoes. Another possibility is to create a windbreak/trellis to protect your pots (just as long as this doesn't backfire and send your cucumbers sailing away over the city).

Wind can also dry out your pots, especially when it's hot. Lay a thick mulch over the soil in your pots to help slow evaporation and to protect the soil from drying out too quickly.

Animals

Animals don't mean to ruin your garden (except for cats, because sometimes cats are jerks), but it happens. Rabbits eat your lettuces and pull the plants out of the soil, roots and all. Deer will browse through your vegetables and your blueberry bushes. Or you'll look out your window and see a squirrel dangling upside down from his toes in your apple tree, a green apple in his gnarled paws. Or there will be a young chicken scratching away in your pot of carrot seedlings, looking for tasty stuff.

To protect your plants from animals, put a wire cage around your plants. If your area is particularly buggy or insect-prone, cover the cage with nylon anti-bug netting, and clip it into place with clothespins. Remove the netting only if you're harvesting tomatoes, adding fertilizers, or pruning. You can even spray for aphids and whiteflies through the netting.

If your pests are larger (birds, chipmunks, squirrels, neighbors) wrap the cage up in bird netting, and maybe one of those motion-sensitive sprinklers nearby that will fire streams of water at the offender.

I can attest that shouting "Get out of that tree, you dang varmit!" through the kitchen window does not deter squirrels in the least. Heaven knows I have tried.

Cheeky little jerk.

Watering

Again – and this is important – make sure your containers have sufficient drainage. If a pot isn't draining, your plants will get root rot. If you suspect that your container is filling up with water, carefully tip the pot over and see if anything pours out. Have the hose handy to wash the poured-out water away, because its putrid smell will knock your socks off.

In the summer, you might have to water once or even twice a day. Use a hose with a sprinkler wand to create a gentle spray of water that will not knock the soil out of the pot.

A layer of mulch in each of your pots will help with watering to some extent, but in the summer heat, your plants' leave will still lose a lot of water through evapotranspiration.

But what happens if you are going to leave for vacation, or if you fall sick, and you can't manage watering? Here are a few ways to nip that in the bud.

Drip Watering System

Set up a drip watering system with a timer to keep the work down. You'd have to spend a couple of bucks to get a drip system, and then it takes a little while to set it up, running all the hoses to each pot, fixing them in place, and then punching the little thingys in the hose so each little thingy drips the water in your flowerpot. Various retailers have drip watering systems for hanging baskets that would work well for container gardening as well. If you set it up with a timer to deliver water every other day, then you can save yourself a little time, and all you have to do is spot-water.

Even with a drip watering system, spot watering will be important, as only one part of the pot gets watered, and if your drip spigot is close to one side of the pot, you'll have to water the other side by hand. One of the greenhouses where I worked had a drip watering system, and occasionally I'd come across a hanging basket with one half staying nice and watered while the other half was bone-dry.

Water-Retaining Soil Additives

Containers generally need more watering than a traditional garden, especially if you have a darker pot, a plant that uses a lot of water, sandy or well-drained soil, or if you use a coir pot that lets the water drain straight out. If your soil is giving you a lot of grief, you can buy a little bag of water-storing crystals, which soak up and retain water. These are used in diapers to the same effect.

Add about a teaspoon of water-storing crystals to a gallon of soil, and put it in at the root level of the plants before adding the rest of the dirt. You won't need a whole lot – and also, if you add too many crystals, they will expand like crazy and push soil out of the top of the pot. Don't ask me how I know this. Just trust me.

Self-Watering Planters

You can get hanging baskets, window boxes, and flowerpots with a water reservoir. Fill the reservoir, and the water wicks out into the pot over a period of several days.

This is a helpful option if you can't always get the watering done on time.

DIY waterers can be as low-tech as a pop bottle, or wine bottle, filled with water and stuck upside-down in the soil. The water slowly leaks out into the soil until the bottle is empty.

Mulch! Mulch!! Mulch!!!

In every gardening book I write, I tend to preach about the benefits of mulch. This book is no exception. The best low-cost or no-cost help that you can get in your garden is a simple layer of mulch on top of the soil. This goes for container gardens as well.

Mulch cools the soil in summer and keeps it insulated in winter. It holds in water. When an organic mulch breaks down, it nourishes the soil. It keeps soil from splashing up on your plant leaves, suppresses weeds, and can make the plant look quite tidy. Overall, it saves you work. I'm always in favor of that.

Organic mulches come in many different forms. You can use grass clippings (make sure they don't have herbicide in them), wood chips, cocoa bean hulls, old sphagnum moss, cardboard bits, newspaper pages torn to fit into your pots. Anything, if it's organic and doesn't contain weed seeds, can go on top of your soil.

Does Companion Planting Really Work?

You can get creative with your containers and plant "theme pots." You might plant an Italian cooking pot (tomato, basil, oregano), a spicy pot (filled with several kinds of ghost and scorpion peppers, eek), or a pot of edible flowers. You can also do rotation gardening with your pots – for instance, lettuce and leafy greens, followed by beans. Again, be sure to choose plants that enjoy the same conditions. For instance, if you're going to put rosemary in a pot, make sure it shares the soil with other plants that also like hot, somewhat dry conditions.

Some plants do well with certain companions. Some plants don't. A good rule of thumb would be to avoid mixing plants from the same family in the same pot because they'd fight for nutrients (as with members of the Apiaceae family: carrots, parsnips, dill, parsley, and fennel) or they'd share diseases between them (as with members of the Solanaceae family: potatoes, tomatoes, peppers, and eggplants).

But I've got to say that outside of these examples, the whole idea of companion planting doesn't hold a lot of water.

Do Carrots Really Love Tomatoes?

Actually, as it turns out, no. Tomatoes aren't actually that crazy about carrots.

Tomato roots release a chemical that apparently keeps pests away from carrots – however, this same chemical also *stunts* carrots, and the effects of this chemical can affect the carrot even a foot and a half away!

So not only do tomatoes not like carrots, but they'd rather keep the carrots at a distance, thank you.

There's probably something to companion gardening, but most of the benefit between plants is simply having plants live in a polycultural setup instead of a monoculture. Nature hates a monoculture. If you have a field all of one plant, she's going to do her best to kill off a bunch of the plants and interseed them with a bunch of weeds. However, when you mix together a bunch of different species in one area, plant health improves overall. Some scientific studies out there indicate that plants are, for the most part, social beings that create communities among themselves, and they prosper when they do.

You can also set up symbiotic relationships between plants in the same pot. Nitrogen-fixing plants such as peas would make leafy vegetables such as lettuce and spinach happy, but they'd have lousy results with root vegetables such as potatoes because the nitrogen they'd add to the soil would make the potato plants all green and lush – at the expense of the potatoes trying to form in the ground.

PART III
GROWING VEGETABLES IN CONTAINERS

At last! The beauty part!

To choose the best container vegetables, read through seed catalogs (which is fun anyway) to find good selections. On seed company websites, do a search for "container plants" or "container" for more choices.

Be sure to choose vegetables that you know your family already enjoys, but feel free to splurge on a few new items just to try them out. Variety is the spice of life.

Herbs, radishes, and greens grow well in shallow containers. Larger plants will need deeper containers. The deepest containers work best for root vegetables (potatoes) and large plants.

I'll include optimal pot sizes in the listings for each vegetable, though these pot sizes are not set in stone. Keep in mind that the more plants you squeeze into a container, the more the yields will decline.

If you find yourself in this pickle, grit your teeth and pull up one of the plants to give the others more space – if you feel that your plant must make this ultimate sacrifice for the greater good!

Cool-Season vs. Warm-Season Crops

In general, your garden plants will fall into two categories: Those that grow best in cool temperatures, and those that grow best in warm temperatures.

Cool-season crops will need to be planted in the early spring, so they can mature before the weather gets too hot. Once the weather heats up, they bolt (bloom) and become tough and bitter. These can also be planted in late summer for a fall harvest, which is trickier but also worthwhile.

Warm-season crops love the heat. If they're put out too early, they'll freeze and die, or be stunted from frost or freezing. But these plants luxuriate in the summer sun and do their best in the heat (with limits – for example, tomatoes stop bearing fruit and drop blossoms when temperatures stay above 90 degrees Fahrenheit).

To make the best of your planting and harvest, be sure to find out the approximate date of your last frost in spring, and the approximate date of your first frost in fall. After the last spring frost (May 15 in Missouri), you can plant your warm-season crops. The first frost date in fall is when you should be finishing your warm-season harvests. Calculate your planting dates accordingly!

Cool-Season Crops

Cool-season vegetables do best in early spring or late fall, and they must be planted early enough to reach maturity before the hot weather hits.

These hardy vegetables can be planted or seeded when temperatures are at least 40 degrees Fahrenheit, though some – such as the semi-hardy plants such as potatoes, cauliflower, and arugula – prefer slightly warmer temperatures.

For best results, start sowing your seeds in batches, staggered a week apart, so if you get abnormally low temperatures one week that freeze your seedlings, you'll have a crop later. Keep sheets or floating row covers handy to cover your young plants during overnight cold snaps and freezes.

Peas

Peas grow well in a 12 to 15-inch pot, or in a long window box. Water peas often, and fertilize them with an all-purpose fertilizer.

You can also grow compact peas in a hanging basket, where they'll flop over the sides of the basket – hopefully you will be tall enough to reach the pea pods when it's time to pick.

You can grow taller varieties in pots if you stake them or give them a trellis to climb on. Be sure to put your trellis or support in the pot before sowing your seeds, to avoid damaging the young sprouts. Plant your peas in a circle in the middle of the pot, spacing them two inches apart. Plant extra peas if you want a really bushy plant.

You can grow peas in early spring, pull them up when the weather heats up and they stop bearing, then plant a crop of leafy hot-weather vegetables to take advantage of the nitrogen that the peas have fixed in the soil.

Also, if you sow several different varieties with different harvest times, you can extend the season. You can also sow a pot of peas, let them start growing, then sow another pot a week or two later. Sow peas from February to March so you can harvest in May; sow them from August to September to harvest in October to November (results may vary).

A Short Primer on Inoculants
Because knowledge is power!

Peas and other legumes (beans, cowpeas, soybeans, alfalfa, etc.) do better if you add a legume seed inoculant to them before planting. This is a pinkish powder that contains rhizobia bacteria. Seeds are coated with this inoculant and planted. When the roots start growing, the bacteria take up residence in the root hairs where they form little nodules that contain bacteria colonies. This is the start of a beautiful friendship, a symbiotic relationship that benefits both. The bacteria gets a safe place to live inside the tissues of the plant roots, as well as energy from photosynthesis. The bacteria convert the nitrogen gas in the soil into ammonia, which is a form of nitrogen that's readily absorbed by the pea plant.

Sometimes you'll get seed peas and beans that are a pinkish color. Those have already been inoculated, so you're good.

Peas sprout and grow when the soil temperature is over 40 degrees F. Use a soil thermometer to check the soil temperature. If you don't have a soil thermometer, an old meat thermometer also works – if you use it only in the garden. (For obvious reasons, please don't use a meat thermometer in the soil and then in your pot roast.)

Container Varieties for Peas

Some of these more compact pea varieties are heirlooms, which is really fun, because not only do you get green peas, but yellow and purple peas as well. They're all cute as buttons and tasty to boot.

Varieties good for containers include Sugar Snap, Little Marvel, Tom Thumb (grows only 8 to 9 inches tall), Early Frosty, Norli, Oregon Sugar Pod, Patio Pride, Avola, Märta (a yellow snow pea), Canoe, Capucijner (a blue-purple heirloom pea from the 1500s), Hurst Green Shaft, Desiree Dwarf Blauwschokkers, Shiraz, and Carouby de Maussane.

Leafy Greens

Spinach and leaf lettuce can be "cut and come again" crops, where you cut off enough for a salad, then let new leaves grow back. When the summer starts heating up, move your leafy greens into partial shade to get a little more use out of them before they bolt and turn bitter. Good spinach varieties for containers include American Viking, Long Standing, Bloomsdale, Melody.

Ico (who does incredible origami art at
https://www.facebook.com/birdbrainorigami/) grew this ginormous Napa cabbage
in a 13-inch pot. Not bad at all!

Cabbage – Any variety is good for containers, but be sure to give each plant enough space to head up. A college buddy grew Napa cabbages on her balcony in containers, and got these gigantic cabbages that could feed hundreds. Well, maybe not hundreds, but close enough.

Arugula – A pot that's 8 inches deep and 6 inches wide works very nicely. A spicy lettuce with edible flowers, arugulas prefer six hours of morning sun, but they don't do well in afternoon heat.

Lettuce – Direct-sow lettuces in containers beginning in late winter, planting them ¼ to ½ inch deep in the soil, 4 to 6 inches apart. Don't let the seedbed dry out while they're germinating. Loose leaf and romaine lettuces need less space than the head lettuce.

Once they start growing, you can sow a new crop every week (or until you run out of pots and/or patience). Succession planting helps stagger the harvest and keeps you from having a glut of lettuce all at once. Also, you can eat baby leaves from the lettuce plants as you thin out the plants. It's all right, they'll make more!

Lettuce can take more shade than other plants,' since they're making leaves instead of flowers and fruit. Shade also helps keep them cool in early summer so they won't bolt so quickly and turn bitter.

Head lettuce takes much longer to mature, about 80 to 95 days, and all those days need to be cool. So that's a challenge!

Looseleaf lettuce is easy to grow, and this lettuce does fine with heat up to a point. Most looseleaf varieties mature in 40 to 45 days.

Romaine lettuce can tolerate some heat and take 70 to 85 days to maturity.

Most any lettuce variety will do fine in containers, but some stellar varieties include Ruby, Buttercrunch, Butterhead, Salad Bowl, Romaine, Dark Green Boston, Bibb, Green Ice, Red Sails, Black Seeded Simpson, Oakleaf, and Deer Tongue.

Broccoli

Use a 2-gallon pot per broccoli plant. DeCicco, Green Comet, Packman, Bonanza, are good varieties.

Beets & Turnips

Most any beets would work in containers, except for mangel beets, which are ginormous. Likewise, turnips are fine in containers, though it's recommended that you grow one turnip per gallon pot. (There's nothing that says you can't plant more, though, to be honest.)

Carrots

Carrots can be grown in something as small as a gallon container that's at least 12 inches deep – just make sure that the pot you choose is two inches deeper than your variety is supposed to grow. Make sure your pot has a drainage hole! Don't keep a saucer under your pot, because the water could collect and give your carrots root rot.

Sow carrot seeds a half-inch apart. Once they come up, thin them to two inches apart. (I'm very bad about thinning carrots alas – my pot is utterly packed with fluffy carrot tops right now. I'll start thinning them when they're a couple of inches long and big enough for nibbling.)

The nice thing about container carrots is that soilless mixes are less pebbly than garden soil, allowing you to grow nice, straight carrots. In pots, you also avoid the soil-borne pests that can show up in regular dirt. Add compost to your soil to make it richer. Harvest carrots before they get too old, so they don't get woody and the roots don't crack.

Add some phosphorus into the soil so the carrots can absorb it directly as they grow. Add perlite for a light, fluffy soil.

Be sure to cover the carrots with a quarter-inch of soil. If the seeds aren't planted deep enough, the carrots' shoulders will show through the top of the soil, turning green instead of orange in the sun. If this happens, spread some extra potting soil over the top until their shoulders are covered up.

Here's an experiment that works in regular soil, that might possibly work in containers: If you have a tough containers that won't be split by frosts, you might be able to raise carrots into the winter. Sow new crops of carrots into mid-fall to give the carrots time to grow roots before frost. Leave them in the ground in your pot and keep them covered so that the container doesn't freeze all the way through. The starches in the carrot turn into sugar in the cold, and then you get sugary carrots into the winter.

Container Varieties for Carrots

To be honest, just about any short carrot variety will do well in containers. I have a few heirloom varieties in this list, so you'll have both orange and yellow varieties. Good container carrots include Danvers Half Long, Short 'n' Sweet,

Tiny Sweet, Scarlet Nantes, Gold Nugget, Little Finger, Baby Spike, Thumbelina, Parisienne, Paris Market, Romeo, Caracas, and Oxheart (this is a chubby, wide carrot, so give it space).

Radishes

Radishes are a sure bet in containers. You can devote whole containers to them, or tuck them in around the edges of other containers while your other plants fill out. Radishes will be fine in a shallow container that's four to six inches deep. Radishes prefer cool weather, but when summer comes, keep them cool by setting them in the shade, and you might be able to coax a longer season out of them. Radish greens are also edible!

Most any radish is good in containers (except for daikon, which needs a deeper container), but some radishes worthy of note include Cherry Belle, Icicle, Scarlet Globe, Champion, Comet, Sparkler, and White Icicle.

Onions and Allies

Onion – White Sweet Spanish, Yellow Sweet Spanish

Green Onions and Garlic – One gallon pot will grow three to five plants. Green onions such as Beltsville Bunching, Crystal Wax, and Evergreen Bunching are good pot varieties.

Warm-Season Crops

Warm-season vegetables are those that are planted after the date of the last frost, preferably after temperatures reach 70 degrees F.

Cool-season crops have two growing seasons – spring and fall – but warm-season crops get summer only and that's it. Once the weather starts getting cold, plant production slows. Tomatoes stay green on the vine instead of ripening, and cucumbers turn bitter. This growing season ends with the first frost in autumn.

Even though warm-season plants love the heat, they still have a rough time in very high temperatures – tomatoes might drop blossoms, and they stop producing fruit when temperatures climb to over 90 degrees Fahrenheit for extended periods of time.

Pole Beans

Once the spring frost and chilly days are over, (in my part of the world, this is after May 15), seed beans directly into your container, at least three or four inches apart and an inch deep.

Some beans mature in 45 days, while others take up to 100 days. Check your calendar and be sure the beans have enough time to mature to harvest before the fall frosts start.

Set up a good-sized trellis. A section of cattle panel fence is extremely sturdy, while round pots might work better with a teepee of three poles tied together at the top.

Pole beans can scramble up 12 to 15-foot trellises with ease. If your trellis is too short, the vines will get to the top, flop over, and climb back down. You'll still be able to reach the beans, mostly. If your vines get to the end of the trellis, you can pinch off the tops (or chop them with shears if they're really getting crazy) to encourage them to branch out from the bottom.

Set up your trellis where it gets 6 to 8 hours of sunlight a day. You can use bamboo, string, wire fencing – whatever the beans can twine around and race up. You can also clip off the weak sprouts that shoot out from the main vines, and cut off the vines that snake behind the trellis and aren't getting any sun.

Pole beans will suck down a lot of water, so you might have to water them daily. (A drip system with a timer can save you some watering time.) They're also hungry plants, so give them a balanced organic water-soluble fertilizer every other week. Mix a little compost into your potting mix to give them moderately rich soil.

If the pole beans develop a spider mite infestation, spray them with a water hose from the front and from the back. And if the leaves are drooping in the hot sun, spray down the leaves with water to cool them off.

Generally beans will grow from 6 to 8 inches long, but pick them while they're small and tender. Keep up with the picking so the plant will keep blooming and bearing beans.

Container Varieties for Pole Beans

Most any pole beans should work in containers. Check the seed packets to see how tall they get, and skip the varieties that are out to eat your house. If you'd like an ornamental pole bean, get Scarlet Runner Pole, which have beautiful red blossoms followed by slender beans that are downright gorgeous.

Bush Beans

These grow best in two-gallon pots, spaced three inches apart. Bush beans can grow in as little as six to seven inches of potting mix, but try to give them a little extra if you can. The growing instructions for these are pretty much the same as the pole beans (above) except without all the trellis work.

Container Varieties for Bush Beans

Good varieties include Blue Lake, Romano, Tender Crop, Topcrop, Greencrop, Contender, Kentucky Wonder, and Derby.

Eggplant

Eggplant are fancy dudes with their purple, white, or yellow fruits. You'll get the best yields when you grow just one plant per two-gallon container, or three eggplants in a 20-inch pot. A mulch of leaves or herbicide-free grass clippings on the soil will help keep water in and keep roots cool.

Eggplants are a hot-weather plant, and they don't like temperatures under 50 degrees F. If you start them inside, don't take them outside until temperatures stay above 50 degrees – or bring their container inside when the temperatures drop.

Stake the plants or put a tomato cage around them when you put the plants out, because even small, compact varieties could use a little support – just like all the rest of us. Pick eggplants by cutting off the stem when they're small and shiny, as the smaller fruits are more tender, and cook them up within a few days. If you keep harvesting them, they'll keep growing them!

Use high-quality, well-draining potting soil with slow-release fertilizer mixed in.

Protip: Fertilize your eggplants every couple of weeks, especially once the blooms start, to help those fruits along. Start your newly-planted eggplant out with a balanced fertilizer – that is, one where all three N-P-K numbers are the same. So, in this case, you could use a 1-1-1 fertilizer or a 20-20-20 one and it's fine. BUT once the eggplant starts flowering, switch over to a high potassium fertilizer for flowering, which has a large final number. 9-15-30 is a good ratio for flowers and fruit.

(HOWEVER if this is too much number stuff to deal with, just use a fertilizer that's specifically formulated for flowering plants. The plant will still be happy with you.)

Flea beetles are a problem for eggplants. These are tiny, black beetles that resemble fleas. They jump out of sight when disturbed, and they pepper the eggplant leaves full of holes. Pyrethrum, an organic insecticide made from chrysanthemums, is a good choice, as is neem oil, but be sure to use these after dark so you don't kill off any bees that are pollinating your plant (the bees fly back to their hives at twilight, so if you spray the plant after the bees clock out for the day, they'll be safe). It's a contact pesticide, so spray it under the leaves where the beetles hide. Squash their tiny larvae on the undersides of the leaves.

Diatomaceous earth is also good, but it only works if it doesn't get wet, and again, you have to keep it away from the blossoms. Also put a yellow trap card close to the lower leaves to catch the flea beetles as they hop from place to place.

Container Varieties for Eggplants

Look for eggplant varieties that are labeled "compact" or "for containers." Compact eggplant varieties include Black Beauty, Ichiban, Slim Jim, Florida Market, Long Tom, Fairy Tale, Hansel, Gretel, Dusky, Crescent Moon, and Bambino.

A dandy Fairy Tale eggplant grown in a container by local librarian Saundra Keiffer.

Peppers

Sow pepper seeds indoors from mid-February to early April to get early transplants. Pepper seedlings like the warmth, so put plastic bags, upside-down jars, or pop bottles cut in half with the lid off, over the seedlings to hold in the heat. When the seed leaves fall off and two true leaves have formed, transplant them into larger pots.

If you pick up your peppers at the nursery, check their tags for specifics on how tall they get. In general, peppers grow well in pots that are at least 14 inches in diameter, one to a pot. Compact varieties might do fine with three in a pot. A five-gallon pot will hold one or two pepper plants, depending on how big they get.

Peppers do well in containers because these warm up quickly when the sun shines on them, and the peppers enjoy heat – up to a point. In intensely hot weather, the peppers need to have their roots shaded from the hot sun. Place the pots in a crate, a planter, or a cardboard box so your pot doesn't overheat, or give it an extra splash of water during the day to cool it off.

If you have a pepper with a spreading growth habit, it probably won't need staking. But it's easier to just give each plant a little grow-through plant hoop, or stick a stake into the soil next to each one, as soon as you plant it, and if you notice that the pepper does need staking, you'll be able to gently stake it with a little piece of twine. (Whichever you choose, install it when you plant, as it's tough to stake a plant after it's been growing for a while. Peppers are somewhat fragile.) Be sure the peppers are protected from strong winds and storms when they're loaded with fruit.

Once the pepper plant is eight inches tall, pinch out the growing tips to get a bushier plant.

Don't let peppers dry out, as they prefer continually moist soil. If your pepper plants wilt, you'll have to water them several times to help them fully recover.

Give the pepper a water-soluble fertilizer every week. A fertilizer formulated for tomatoes would be a good choice, but any balanced fertilizer is fine as long as it includes calcium and magnesium – these are nutrients that the pepper needs for good fruit set.

Organic fertilizers that are good for peppers include fish emulsion, greensand (this is a soil supplement made from ancient undersea deposits that's high in iron, potassium, and magnesium, as well as trace nutrients), kelp meal, and bone meal. Research indicates that seaweed supplements (i.e. kelp) are great additions to any regular fertilizer regimen.

When fruit starts maturing, you might spray the plant with a liquid copper fungicide to help prevent bacterial rots. Always read and follow label instructions.

When the time comes to harvest, leave the peppers on the plant until they are fully colored, then pick them promptly. Leaving overripe fruit on the plant slows down production, and letting fruit rot on the plant could start rot in other peppers.

Container Varieties for Peppers

Choose a pepper with small fruits and a bushy habit. Pepper varieties that are labeled as "compact" or "for containers" are a good choice, as regular pepper varieties can get out of control in a smaller pot.

Hot peppers: Cayenne, Long Red, Red Cherry, Jalapeno, Red Chilli, Super Chili, Cheyenne F1, Italico, Zavory, Yellow Mushroom, Red Mushroom, Orange Thai, and Big Thai.

Sweet (bell) peppers: Redskin, Mohawk; Spicy Pepper Apache, Cupid, Redskin, Camelot, Jupiter, Sweet Banana, Wonder, Yolo Wonder, Keystone Resistant Giant, Gourmet, Canape, Lady Bell, Gypsy, Crispy, New Ace, and Oda.

Tomatoes

Large 20-inch plastic pots with saucers are a good bet for these tomatoes. Plastic pots are easy to move, store, and sanitize at the end of the season.

Here's a way to get an early jump on the season, if you want to plant your tomato before the last spring frost. Plant your tomato plant deep in the pot. Put a few inches of soil at the bottom, set your tomato plant in there, then fill up the pot until only the top five inches of your tomato plant is sticking out. So if you have a big pot, it will be half-filled with soil with a tiny little sprout peeking out.

It looks funny, but here's the beauty part. Set the pot in the warmest place in your yard, then lay a sheet of Plexiglas or any transparent plastic over the top. Behold! You have made a miniature greenhouse for your tomato.

As the tomato grows, keep adding soil to fill in around the plant. Do this until you've filled the pot with soil (leave two inches of headroom so the pot can hold the water you give to the tomato). The tomato will develop roots all along its stem, making it sturdy and strong, and all those roots are absorbing all those nutrients you added to the soil.

By the way, plant only one tomato per pot. If it's competing with another tomato, it's not going to do as well.

Fill the pot up with soil to two inches from the top. Then put in a cage made of concrete reinforcing wire, or whatever stake, trellis, or cage system you want to use to support your plant.

Also add a layer of mulch to the pot to keep the moisture in, to keep roots cool in the summer sun, and to keep little weeds from popping up in the potting soil.

Feed your tomatoes with liquid fertilizer such as fish emulsion, Miracle Gro, compost tea, or whichever fertilizer you prefer, about once a month to keep the plants healthy and the tomatoes.

Do you see a stem on your tomato that is not bearing flowers or fruit? Pinch it off. Then the tomato can divert energy toward fruits. Also, pinching off the suckers will give you a stronger, bushier plant in general.

At the end of the season, when the frost hits and the tomatoes are finished, dump the potting soil into the garden, throw away the Styrofoam peanuts, and clean the pots out and scrub them with a bleach solution to get rid of any insect eggs or diseases that might be harbored there. Then put them in the garage and wait for next spring to start afresh.

Container Varieties for Tomatoes

Any tomato variety with the word "Patio" in its name is probably a sure bet. Good varieties include Black Seaman, Patio Princess, Czech's Bush, Sophie's Choice, Silver Fir Tree (also a pretty little tomato plant), Bushsteak (big tomatoes on a little plant), Whippersnapper (its size and yield depend on the size of the container you put it in), Sweetheart on the Patio (cherry tomatoes), Marglobe, Baxter's Bush Cherry, Gardener's Delight (also an heirloom, so you can save the seeds from year to year), Balcony, Bush Early Girl, Stupice, Tumbling Tom Yellow, Small Fry, Sweet 100, Tiny Tim, Micro Tom, Minibel, Pixie, Saladette, Toy Boy, Spring Giant. Jetstar, Celebrity, and Super Bush are full-sized tomatoes that would also work in a container.

Potatoes

Container-grown potatoes won't get as big or yield as much as those grown in the soil, but they're still fresh potatoes, and they still taste good. What's more, these potatoes should be protected against the various soil-borne fungus or blight diseases that in-ground potatoes are sometimes subjected to.

Early-season potatoes, which mature within 75 to 90 days, and mid-season potatoes, maturing between 95 and 110 days, are good in containers. You can dig out the whole crop after the potato plants turn yellow and die, or you can carefully dig into your soil before harvest and bring up some new potatoes for an early treat.

Mid and late-season potatoes (120 to 135 days) can be good choices because they'll form tubers over a long period of time – but you'll need a long growing season for these. Make sure you'll be able to harvest them before the first frost of fall.

Potatoes will need large containers – at least 16 inches wide and deep. A 10-gallon pot also works. The 16x16 container can be planted with four to six seed potatoes. You can fill a large storage container (with excellent drainage) with finely chopped leafmold or straw instead of soil to plant the potatoes. This allows you to harvest new potatoes easily, and they also come out clean.

A five-gallon bucket with a hole drilled in the bottom will hold one to two seed potatoes. You can buy grow bags for potatoes, which have flaps on their sides that allow you to reach into the soil and pull out some potatoes without having to dig around. A half-barrel with drainage is also good, or you can use a storage container with holes punched in the bottom.

Prepare the seed potatoes before you plant them. Twenty-four or 48 hours before planting, cut the large seed potatoes into pieces, each piece with one or two eyes. Each eye will grow into a new potato plant. Smaller seed potatoes can be planted whole. Then let the cut pieces cure (i.e. dry out) until planting.

To plant the potatoes, lay six inches of potting soil with granular fertilizer in the bottom of the container. (Don't use lime, which encourages scab to grow on your potatoes.) Lay the seed potatoes on top, six inches (15 cm) apart. Cover them with six more inches of soil and keep them watered. When the new sprouts grow over six inches tall, add more soil to the container. Repeat the process until the container is nearly full. Leave about six inches of foliage exposed so the plant can keep producing the sugars and carbohydrates that the tubers need. The potatoes will develop off the sides of the stem.

Mulch them well, which will keep any sunlight off the tubers (sunlight on the tubers make them green and toxic) and also keeps the soil moist. Potatoes will grow best in a moist (not soggy) soil.

Potatoes need a full day of sun. However, they stop growing when the temperature reaches the high 80s. On hot days, help them by shading them during the hottest part of the day but exposing them to morning and afternoon sun.

Give the potatoes a soluble fertilizer while the foliage is growing. Manure or compost tea is good, as well as kelp meal and bone meal.

When the potato plants turn yellow, or when the tops of the plants start to die back, your potatoes are ready to be dug up. Stop watering and let the foliage dry out, and then you can tip the container onto a tarp and retrieve your 'taters. Handle them gently because they'll bruise easily, and let them dry in a cool, dark location, like a root cellar or basement. Don't wash them until you're ready to use them.

Container Varieties for Potatoes

Early potatoes: Chieftain, Dark Red Norland, Irish Cobbler, Sangre, Red Gold, and Yukon Gold.

Fingerling potatoes: AmaRosa, Banana, French Fingerling, Pinto, and Rose Finn Apple.

Summer Squash and Zucchini

Plant the bush varieties, not the vines. One plant per 24-inch pot, or per five-gallon pot. Technically, you can plant squash and zucchini in a 12-inch pot, so if that's all you have, you should be fine. A trellis in the pot will help keep the plant off the ground.

If you grow winter squash, make sure you choose a compact variety, so you're not surprised by your mystery plant suddenly popping out a 20-pound squash in the middle of your deck.

Container Varieties for Various Squashes
Summer squash: Dixie, Gold Neck, Early Prolific Straightneck, Bush Crookneck.

Zucchini: Black Magic, Diplomat, Senator.

Acorn squash: Honey Bear, Bush Acorn.

Cucumbers

For cucumbers, use a one-gallon pot per plant. These guys love warm soil, and containers that sit in the summer sun will make your cukes just as happy as can be. (All the same, protect the pot from scorching temperatures.) Bush cucumbers are more compact but they also give you smaller yields compared to a vining cucumber. If you choose a vining cucumber, put a trellis or some kind of framework into the pot for them to grow up on.

Keep their soil moist and feed them every other week, because they're hungry plants.

Keep a close eye on the cucumbers, because it doesn't take long for a tasty little cucumber to turn enormous, overripe, and bitter. Snip them off the vine when you harvest to avoid damaging the vine.

Container Varieties for Cucumbers

Good container varieties include Patio Pik, Pot Luck, Spacemaster, Burpless, Liberty, Early Pik, Crispy, Salty, Salad Bush, Lemon Cucumber (it's yellow, lemon-shaped, and cute!), Bush Champion, Diva, and Northern Pickling.

Muskmelons & Cantaloupe

I've been using these two terms interchangeably, but apparently muskmelon is the type of melon that cantaloupes and other melons have been derived from. I am writing this paragraph in the eleventh hour of editing so my understanding of this etymological conundrum might not be correct, and will be updated later – but as a side note, this is yet another reason why I shouldn't procrastinate.

Cantaloupes grow best in containers with 5 gallons or more of potting soil. If you have an extra tote container that you're not using, then repurpose it, put some drainage holes in it, and plop one or two melons in there.

The problem with melons and cantaloupe plants is that they take up a lot of garden space with their vines – but if you can find some small-fruited varieties and grow them up a trellis, you'll be able to fit garden melons into your balcony landscape. Even better, when you grow the vines up, you keep the melons off the ground, away from pests and rot.

Set your container up next to your trellis. Add compost and organic fertilizer to the soil, plant your seeds, and as the new plants come up, help guide them onto the trellis so the tendrils take hold of the netting or wire. Keep the seedlings watered and fertilize them every other week, because these guys need nourishment. Mulch the soil to keep the roots cool and hold moisture in.

If you're growing melons on a trellis, make slings out of old T-shirts to help support their weight so they don't break off the vine before they're ripe.

Container Varieties for Melons

Many of these are small-sized melons that will fit into your hand, and they're early producers. Sugar Cube, Honey Bun, Minnesota Midget (bush type), Tasty Bites, Tigger (the cutest, craziest melon you'll meet), Green Machine, Charentais, Alvaro, Golden Jenny, Early Silver Line, Kazakh, Top Mark, and Sprite.

Watermelon

These are tough to grow in pots, as watermelon vines can grow up to ten feet long. But there's no crying in gardening! We can make it work!

Compact varieties work best, for obvious reasons. A large pot is good for this endeavor. Get a pot that won't lose a lot of water, such as a plastic or glazed pot, and choose a good-quality potting soil amended with some finished compost and some granular fertilizer.

Sow one to three watermelon seeds per container, one inch deep.

Once the plants start growing, keep the soil moist until the watermelons are all harvested. Don't let the soil dry out, as the repeated practice of letting the soil dry out and then watering heavily will cause the watermelons to crack, diluting their flavor. You might need to water them once or even twice a day, or you can set up a drip system and supplement that with extra water when needed.

Give them a drink of fertilizer every two to three weeks.

Choose a watermelon variety that yields small fruits, so you can grow them on a sturdy trellis or a tough tomato cage. Weave the vines through the wire mesh to train them up the trellis, and tie the vines to the trellis if necessary.

Once the fruit starts to develop, use an old T-shirt or old nylon hose, or any kind of stretchy material, to make a sling or hammock to support the growing fruits.

Self-pollination

Watch your fruits as they start to form. If the tiny watermelons keep falling off the vine, you'll have to self-pollinate your flowers.

Here's how it works: Watermelons have both male and female flowers. The male flowers have a fuzzy stalk, i.e. the stamen, in the middle of the flower; while the female flower has a mini-watermelon at its base and a stigma in the middle of the flower. Use a paintbrush, or a cotton swab, to pick the pollen up from the stamen, then brush the pollen against the sticky stigma. When your paintbrush is out of pollen, brush off some more and keep transferring it. Or, pick the male flower and brush it up against every stigma you can find on the plant. Do this every couple of days while the new flowers are opening. You can pollinate flowers more than once – after all, the bees do. This work should bear fruit, literally.

The melons are ripe when they develop a yellow spot on one side. Also, look at the curly little tendrils next to where the watermelon is attached. When those tendrils turn brown and die, that indicates your melon is ready for harvesting. Clip the stem – don't pull the melon off. Wait until the melon is fully ripened before picking because they will not ripen off the vine.

Container Varieties for Watermelons

Sugar Baby Bush is a dwarf bush vine whose vines grow only 3 ½ feet long. Black Tail Mountain and Sugar Pot are also small varieties that you can grow on a trellis. Have slings handy to support the melons.

Berries

Berry plants need at least six to eight hours of sunlight a day, and they'll need to be watered daily or every other day if there's no rain.

Plant berries in a container that is 20 to 36 inches wide and deep, such as five-gallon pots or half-barrels. Three to six raspberry canes in one such pot, or one blueberry bush, is sufficient. Avoid using terracotta or ceramic pots for berries as these pots occasionally break during the winter freeze-thaw cycle.

In winter, move the berry pots to an unheated garage or some sheltered place (heavily mulch the pots if you can't move them) and let them go dormant, watering them twice a month if they're in a place where they don't get rain (the plants are dormant but the roots are still growing).

Rhubarb

Obviously not a berry, but I am placing rhubarb next to the strawberries in this book because that's how you make a pie.

Rhubarb is a perennial, which means it will come back year after year. These guys can live for 15 to 20 years if you treat it well, though generally it won't last this long in a container. Start with providing rich potting mix, amended generously with well-rotted manure or compost. This is a big plant with a big root system, so plant your rhubarb in a pot that allows it to stretch and grow, such as a half-barrel.

Container rhubarb won't give you huge yields, but it should give you a couple of pies, which is worthwhile.

In spring, remove all flowers so the plant's energy is directed into the stems. Feed it every other week, and keep it watered in summer – don't let the soil dry out. In fall, after the leaves die back, cut back the stalks, mulch with compost and leaves (leave the crown uncovered so it doesn't rot), and put it inside an unheated shed, or if it's on a balcony, keep it covered over the winter, and water it occasionally.

Strawberries

These are great pot plants. A pot that's 18 inches wide and 8 inches deep is good, though hanging baskets and strawberry jars are great. Any container that is wider than it is deep will be a good choice here. Plant them about 10 inches apart, keeping the roots covered with soil but keep the crown of the plant above the soil to avoid crown rot. You should have six to 10 berry plants per person.

Avoid overcrowding them – so no more than three plants per square foot of soil. They're shallow-rooted, so you don't need a deep pot, but space really helps them thrive.

You'll want the strawberries to keep bearing, so snip off all runner plants they put out while the strawberries are blooming and setting fruit.

Once fruiting season is over, let runners root in different parts of the pot to replace any strawberry plants that are sick or old. Fertilize your plants with compost or an organic balanced fertilizer, because now that they've stopped fruiting, they're already preparing the buds and blossoms for next year's flowers in the crown of the plant. (These are called perennating buds.) Encouraging healthy plants allows these buds to give you healthy blooms next year. If the plant starves and loses these buds, it will still bloom next year, but not as generously.

At any rate, as fall stretches into winter, give your strawberry plants one last dose of fertilizer – something low in nitrogen (you don't want to encourage them to put out soft, green leaves just before a cold snap hits) but high in phosphorus and potassium. When the days turn short and cold, overwinter the strawberry pots in an unheated garage or shed, or mulch the pots well, or wrap them in some insulating material, and water them occasionally to keep them alive. They'll need this period of dormancy to start blooming and fruiting next spring.

Container Varieties for Strawberries

If you live in a cool area with cool summers, day-neutral strawberries such as Tribute, Tristar, and Seascape are likely your best choices. These are everbearing strawberries that are bear fruit more consistently through the year. Day-neutral strawberries stop bearing in hot weather, so these are more for our northern neighbors.

Everbearing strawberries bear fruit twice a year – Ozark Beauty, Tillicum, and Quinalut are three good choices. June-bearing strawberries aren't good for containers as they bear only in June and then berry season is over.

Raspberries

Many of these are too big to be grown in containers, but smaller and dwarf varieties include Heritage, Raspberry Shortcake (this one is thornless!), and Fall Gold. Raspberries are perennials that set fruit on two-year-old canes (they'll give you a few berries in year one but the second year is when they really start fruiting.) Every spring, new green shoots come up and these will be next year's fruiting canes. When your two-year old canes are done fruiting, cut them down and let the new canes take their place. Cut off dead canes at ground level.

Blueberries

Blueberries have a number of different species which are grown in a number of temperate zones. *Vaccinium angustifolia* and *V. corymbosum* are mostly northern species, though the latter can be grown clear down in Georgia, while the rabbiteye blueberry, *Vaccinium virgatum*, also known as *V. ashei*, grows best in the southeastern United States.

You'll likely need to get two blueberry plants for improved pollination.

Blueberries are in the Ericaceae family, a plant family that grow best in acidic soil. Your berries will need a potting-soil mix for acid-loving plants with a pH balance between 4.5 and 5.5. They won't need a whole lot of fertilizer – apply an organic fertilizer in low doses two or three times through the year.

Mulch the blueberries, two to three inches deep – pine bark mulch is a good choice because it's acidic and breaks down over time to add fertility to the soil. Feel free to add coffee grounds and tea bags to the blueberry's mulch occasionally – you don't even have to make them a pot of coffee.

Give blueberry bushes 6 to 8 hours of sunlight daily – keep the soil moist but make sure the pot is draining well. Add some sand to your peat mixture to improve drainage.

Add 2 tablespoons of apple cider vinegar to a gallon of water in your watering pot and use this to add a little acidity and some micronutrients to your blueberry's soil.

Have some light netting to throw over the plants when they're fruiting, or you'll be engaged in a battle royale with robins and catbirds over the berries.

Dwarf hybrid blueberries have become very popular, naturally. Sunshine Blue, Top Hat, and Jelly Bean are three good varieties for container growing.

The End!

I hope you enjoyed the book! Please leave an honest review for this book on Amazon, BookBub, or Goodreads.

Reviews are so helpful to authors and to the readers who are looking for good book recommendations.

Thus endeth the first book of the Hungry Garden series.

If you enjoyed this book – and I hope you did! – preorder the next book in the series:

Edible Landscaping – Grow a Food Forest Through Permaculture

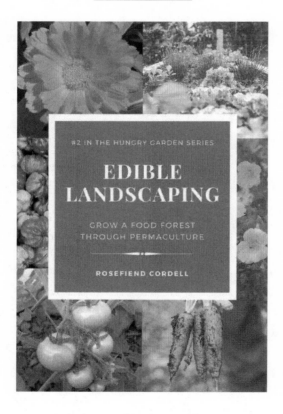

Preorder on Amazon!!

Me in February 2018 with two baby chickies, my laptop, and a can of Red Bull.
This is how I roll, people.

ABOUT THE AUTHOR

A former city horticulturist and a long-time garden writer, Rosefiend Cordell, aka Melinda R. Cordell, has written 12 books in the Easy-Growing Gardening series under the name Rosefiend Cordell.

She's worked in horticulture for half of her life – longer if you count when she was young, collecting wildflowers. She's worked in greenhouses, both retail and commercial; as a landscape laborer and designer, as a perennials manager, as municipal horticulturist and public rose garden potentate, and now as a gardening author (which is much easier on the back and joints).

Melinda R. Cordell has written a truckload of YA novels, including the Dragonriders of Skala series (like *Game of Thrones*, with Vikings), and now she's releasing the Dragonriders of Fiorenza series. Set in an alternative medieval Italy, it features a wily dragonrider, her loyal dragon, and her assassin grandma, all pitted against a world out to strip away every last one of their hopes and 3dreams.

Melinda lives in northwest Missouri with her husband and two kids, the best little family to walk the earth, and is writing about 24 books at once, fueled by passion and caffeine.

If you want to keep up with her, click here to get a free book of gardening tips. Or you can drop her a friendly note at rosefiend@gmail.com.

Don't forget to leave a book review on Amazon, BookBub, or Goodreads!

melindacordell.com

Made in the USA
Middletown, DE
17 August 2020